Introduction

Discover the potential in this great inexpensive and easy form of pupp~~, the very hearts of people.

Twelve ready to use scripts for the Solo Puppeteer and Scruff (PB-01G Dog in the Bag Puppet). It will take you just a few minutes to teach Children and Adults too, some very important Bible truths in a fun way.

CONTENTS

SCRUFFY - TO BOLDLY GO (GIDEON)

Hello Scruffy, how are you today? **(Scruffy looks around mouth open)**
Scruffy, what's the matter? **(Scruffy whispers)**
What have I done to my hair? **(Scruffy nods)**
Well I have been to the hairdresser's **(Scruffy whispers)**
Was he out? **(Scruffy nods)**
Oh Scruffy, you horror! **(Scruffy laughs)**
No come on; tell me what you've been up to lately. **(Scruffy whispers)**
There's a new dog moved in up the road. **(Scruffy nods)**
What's he like? **(Scruffy whispers)**
You don't know? **(Scruffy shakes his head)**
Why's that? **(Scruffy whispers)**
You haven't spoken to him yet. **(Scruffy shakes his head)**
Why not? **(Scruffy whispers)**
He might be fierce. **(Scruffy nods)**
Well I'm sure his bark is worse than his bite. **(Scruffy whispers)**
That's what you're afraid of. **(Scruffy nods)**
Oh Scruffy I know you don't like noise but you could be missing out on making a new friend. **(Scruffy whispers)**
He might not want to be friendly. **(Scruffy shakes his head, Scruffy whispers)**
You thought you might go and have a look at him in disguise. **(Scruffy nods)**
What do you mean? **(Scruffy retrieves a wig from his bag)**
What's this? It's a blond wig. Lets try it on you. **(Put it on Scruffy's head)** Oh Scruffy you do look funny. Anyway I thought dogs knew who they were talking to by their smell. **(Scruffy looks around mouth open)** Let's take it off. **(Scruffy whispers)**
It was a bit hot. **(Scruffy nods)**
Well Scruffy you won't find out if he's friendly unless you go and speak to him. You know what they say - "To Boldly Go" **(Scruffy shakes his head)**
What do you mean "no"? **(Scruffy whispers)**
They might have split the atom, but you're sure I shouldn't split the infinitive? **(Scruffy nods)**
Oh Scruffy! **(Scruffy whispers)**
It's all right for me because I'm big? **(Scruffy nods)**
Shall I tell you a story about someone God helped in the bible? **(Scruffy nods, Scruffy whispers)**
You like stories. **(Scruffy nods)**
This man was called Gideon. In those days they had lots of fierce enemies and so Gideon and his people used to go and hide in caves. **(Scruffy whispers)**
Could I tell you where the caves are because that sounds like a good idea? **(Scruffy nods)**
They are a long way from here, Scruffy, in a place called Israel. **(Scruffy looks around mouth open)**

One day an Angel of the Lord came and called Gideon a mighty warrior. **(Scruffy whispers)**
He wasn't really because he was behaving like a scaredy cat. **(Scruffy nods)**
A bit like you, Scruffy? (Scruffy looks around mouth open, **Scruffy whispers)**
You'd never behave anything like a cat. **(Scruffy shakes his head)**
Then God gave Gideon the courage to call an army of 32,000 men together. **(Scruffy whispers)**
That sounds like a lot of men to fight their enemies. **(Scruffy nods)**
But God said there were too many men. **(Scruffy looks around mouth open)**
And he told Gideon to tell those who were afraid to go home. **(Scruffy whispers)**
That would have been you? **(Scruffy nods)**
That left 10,000 men and God still said it was too many. **(Scruffy looks around mouth open)**
So God told Gideon to tell the men to drink from a stream, and any who lapped like dogs were to be sent home. **(Scruffy whispers)**
You're glad you're a dog. **(Scruffy nods)**
There were only 300 men left with Gideon. **(Scruffy looks around mouth open)**
God told them to go on the hillsides surrounding their enemies at night with a trumpet each and a torch inside a jar. **(Scruffy whispers)**
No weapons? **(Scruffy nods)**
That's right, Scruffy, no weapons. **(Scruffy looks around mouth open)**
When Gideon gave the signal, his men all blew their trumpets, shouted "A sword for the Lord and for Gideon", broke the jars, and waved the flaming torches. **(Scruffy whispers)**
You would have gone to hide because of all the noise. **(Scruffy nods)**
Well the enemies were so frightened and confused that they all started killing each other in the dark, and the ones who were left, ran away. **(Scruffy whispers)**
What happened then? **(Scruffy nods)**
Gideon and his men gave chase and defeated them and there was peace for 40 years; the rest of Gideon's lifetime. **(Scruffy whispers)**
So God made him a mighty warrior? **(Scruffy nods)**
That's right Scruffy, God did.
Do you know, Scruffy, that when I first came to church with you just over a year ago, I was very frightened? **(Scruffy whispers)**
So were you. **(Scruffy nods)**
But as I have prayed, God has helped me and inspired me and I've been so grateful to Him. "For God did not give us a spirit of timidity, but a spirit of power, of love and of self-discipline."
We don't have to hide (hold up the wig) and pretend to be something we're not ....and do you know I've had an awful lot of fun!

So do you think you could go and speak to that new dog now? **(Scruffy hides his head, Scruffy whispers)**

You might walk past his gate wearing your football scarf? **(Scruffy nods)**

That's a good idea, but what happens if he doesn't support your team? **(Scruffy whispers)**

Of course any self-respecting dog would support your team. **(Scruffy nods)**

Oh Scruffy! **(Scruffy starts to disappear inside his bag)** Hey where are you off to? **(Scruffy whispers)**

You've had an idea. **(Scruffy nods, Scruffy whispers)**

You're going to dig up your third best bone and offer to share it with him. **(Scruffy nods and disappears)**

Mind my garden bulbs, **please**.

SCRUFFY - THE PRODIGAL

Scruffy, are you in there? **(Scruffy shakes his head from inside the bag)**
No! What do you mean "no"? **(Scruffy's nose appears and he whispers)**
You're an older and wiser dog? **(Scruffy comes out of his bag and nods slowly)**
Scruffy, what has happened to you? **(Scruffy whispers)**
You were told off for jumping up to the kitchen surface and finishing off a chocolate bar that was just asking to be eaten. **(Scruffy nods, Scruffy whispers)**
How were you to know someone still wanted it? **(Scruffy nods, Scruffy whispers)**
If you're given any food, especially treats, you wolf it down straight away. **(Scruffy nods)**
So what happened then? **(Scruffy whispers)**
You went into a corner and sulked. **(Scruffy nods, Scruffy whispers)**
And then you had a bright idea. **(Scruffy nods, Scruffy whispers)**
You collected up all the dog biscuits and Good Boy Choc Drops you could find. **(Scruffy nods, Scruffy whispers)**
You put them in your bag and waited until the door was left open that evening and then you sneaked out. **(Scruffy nods)**
Where did you go? **(Scruffy whispers)**
Where the lights were brightest and where things seemed to be happening. **(Scruffy nods)**
So what did you do? **(Scruffy whispers)**
You sniffed at all the interesting smells. **(Scruffy nods, Scruffy whispers)**
There were so many of them, you just didn't know which one to follow next. **(Scruffy nods, Scruffy whispers)**
Suddenly you realized you were being watched. **(Scruffy nods, Scruffy whispers)**
It was some of the members of the Terrible Terrier Troupe, and as you looked, more arrived and you were surrounded. **(Scruffy nods)**
Oh Scruffy, weren't you frightened? **(Scruffy nods and begins to tremble)**
What happened next? **(Scruffy whispers)**
They got closer and closer. **(Scruffy nods, Scruffy whispers)**
Then one of them asked if you were hungry. **(Scruffy nods, Scruffy whispers)**
So you told them all about the biscuits and the chocolate. **(Scruffy nods, Scruffy whispers)**
They became really friendly and asked you to show them. **(Scruffy nods, Scruffy whispers)**
So you got some out of your bag. **(Scruffy nods)**
What happened then? **(Scruffy whispers)**
They said it would be a good idea to count what you'd got. **(Scruffy nods)**
So what did you do? **(Scruffy whispers)**

You put your head in your bag to get out some more things. **(Scruffy nods, Scruffy whispers)**

But when you looked up, there seemed to be less than you thought. **(Scruffy nods, Scruffy whispers)**

Then they asked you if you'd like to share what you'd got as you had so much and they were hungry. **(Scruffy nods, Scruffy whispers)**

So you did. **(Scruffy nods, Scruffy whispers)**

But a bag full of food doesn't go very far among so many. **(Scruffy nods, Scruffy whispers)**

When it was all gone, they didn't seem so friendly any more. **(Scruffy nods, Scruffy whispers)**

Particularly when you told them you didn't think you'd be able to get any more. **(Scruffy nods, Scruffy whispers)**

As they left, they pushed past you and you fell over into a muddy puddle. **(Scruffy nods, Scruffy whispers)**

You were still hungry as they hadn't let you eat very much and now you were cold and wet as well. **(Scruffy nods, Scruffy whispers)**

You saw some dogs nosing round some dustbins. **(Scruffy nods, Scruffy whispers)**

But when you went to investigate, it was cold overcooked cabbage. **(Scruffy nods, Scruffy whispers)**

You went up on your hind legs to look in lots of windows. **(Scruffy nods, Scruffy whispers)**

All the people inside seemed happy and warm and lots of them were eating lovely food. **(Scruffy nods, Scruffy whispers)**

You sat down and started to howl. **(Scruffy nods)**

Oh Scruffy, did anyone hear you? **(Scruffy shakes his head, Scruffy whispers)**

You suddenly realized that home was not such a bad place after all. **(Scruffy nods, Scruffy whispers)**

In fact it was a pretty good place. **(Scruffy nods, Scruffy whispers)**

You realized you'd been very foolish and thought you'd better go home and see if you were still in the doghouse. **(Scruffy nods, Scruffy whispers)**

You realized you were going to be in a lot of trouble. **(Scruffy nods, Scruffy whispers)**

But Jake met you on the way and told you that everyone was out looking for you. **(Scruffy nods, Scruffy whispers)**

And that they were very worried about you. **(Scruffy nods, Scruffy whispers)**

You hadn't realized that you'd be cared for that much. **(Scruffy nods)**

Oh Scruffy, of course you're cared for.

(*To audience*) We too are loved so much by God.

Jesus says "Behold, I stand at the door and knock, if anyone hears my voice and opens the door I will come in and eat with him and he with me."

He wants us to come and be reconciled to him but he doesn't force himself on us.

No matter what we've done, He is prepared to forgive us.

He is always searching us out.
Well Scruffy, you won't ever do that again will you? **(Scruffy shakes his head slowly)**
Even if you do get told off, you know you're very much loved.
(Scruffy nods and disappears inside his bag.)

Scruffy - Thank You

Good Morning Scruffy, last time you came to see us you were feeling a bit sad because you'd missed out on your holiday, weren't you? **(Scruffy nods, Scruffy whispers)**
You're feeling quite perky today? **(Scruffy nods)**
What have you been up to lately? **(Scruffy whispers)**
You've been to Toddlers. **(Scruffy nods)**
You saw, b and c there. **(Scruffy nods)** *(It always has more impact if you mention names of people who are present.)*
Was it fun there? **(Scruffy nods, Scruffy whispers)**
You thought you'd like to get a part time job there. **(Scruffy nods)**
What sort of job did you think you could have at Toddlers? **(Scruffy whispers)**
As a cleaner. **(Scruffy nods)**
Scruffy, it's a very big job clearing up at the end of Toddlers. **(Scruffy whispers)**
It wasn't that. **(Scruffy shakes his head)**
What job did you think you could do? **(Scruffy whispers)**
Some of the children drop their biscuits. **(Scruffy nods, Scruffy whispers)**
That was the part of the time you wanted to help. **(Scruffy nods)**
I see. **(Scruffy whispers)**
You wanted to say a big thank you to the little girl who came up and put a blanket round you and gave you a big hug. **(Scruffy nods)**
Wasn't that kind? **(Scruffy nods, Scruffy whispers)**
You've also been doing some Contact visiting. **(Scruffy nods)**
What's Contact visiting? **(Scruffy whispers)**
When people get a bit older they can't get out and about as they used to. **(Scruffy nods, Scruffy whispers)**
Some of them can't even get to church. **(Scruffy nods)**
So you go and see them. Do you like that? **(Scruffy whispers)**
They tell you lots of interesting things. **(Scruffy nods, Scruffy whispers)**
Some of them make a fuss of you. **(Scruffy nods, Scruffy whispers)**
Some of them have never seen you before. **(Scruffy nods, Scruffy whispers)**
And there are biscuits. **(Scruffy nods, Scruffy whispers)**
You want to say "hello" to Mrs B and "thank you" for the ginger biscuits. **(Scruffy nods, Scruffy whispers)**
And you've had a postcard. **(Scruffy nods)**
Have you Scruffy, who is it from? **(Scruffy whispers)**
You can't read. **(Scruffy nods and retrieves it from his bag)**
Oh, you've brought it with you. It's a picture of a large ship on a field. **(Scruffy whispers)**
It looks safe to travel on. **(Scruffy nods)**
Shall I read it out to you? **(Scruffy nods)**
It's from someone who's been to America. It says "They eat hot

dogs over here." **(Scruffy looks round open mouthed, then whispers)**
You're feeling a bit cold. **(Scruffy nods, Scruffy whispers)**
You want to go back in your bag. **(Scruffy trembles and nods)**
Oh no Scruffy, it doesn't mean they're eating real dogs, it's what they call sausages. **(Scruffy whispers)**
You like sausages. **(Scruffy nods)**
Shall I read on? It says "there are no cats here". **(Scruffy whispers)**
That sounds even better. **(Scruffy nods)**
"There are lots of trees." **(Scruffy whispers)**
Trees are very important. **(Scruffy nods)**
Why are trees very important Scruffy? **(Scruffy looks round open mouthed, then whispers)**
Because of the ozone layer. **(Scruffy nods)**
Scruffy, do you know what the ozone layer is? **(Scruffy whispers)**
You think it's a pop group. **(Scruffy nods)**
Never mind Scruffy, I'm sure you'll find out what it is one day. Shall I tell you who sent you the card? **(Scruffy whispers)**
You don't want to embarrass them so you want me to whisper it in your ear. **(Scruffy nods)**
(*Lift up Scruffy's ear and whisper the person's name (A) loudly*)
(Scruffy whispers)
You'll give "A" a big lick afterwards to say thank you. **(Scruffy nods)**
Well that's three, "thank you's" you've said today, Scruffy. **(Scruffy nods, Scruffy whispers)**
You want to find out what it's like when people say "thank you" to you. **(Scruffy nods)** (*If there is anyone in the congregation with a special birthday or anniversary etc. then Scruffy could give out a card here.*)
(Scruffy whispers)
So you want some of the children to come up so that you can give them something. **(Scruffy nods)**
Scruffy, it's not a trick is it? **(Scruffy shakes his head)**
You're not going to give them dog biscuits are you? **(Scruffy shakes his head, Scruffy whispers)**
Something that children like? **(Scruffy nods)**

(Invite the children up. (*NB I placed ten mats on the floor beforehand and invited the children up in age order to avoid a stampede. I did this because we were studying the story of the ten lepers in Sunday Club that day. If you can somehow arrange it so that 'A', who wrote the postcard, is one of the ten then so much the better as the audience will love it.*) **(Scruffy gets a bag of sweets out of his bag)**
What have you got in there, Scruffy? Oh, it's sweets. You haven't been licking them have you? **(Scruffy whispers)**
You couldn't get the wrappers off. **(Scruffy nods)**
(Scruffy gives out the sweets. Encourage the children to say "Thank you" if they forget.)
How did that make you feel Scruffy, to hear all those children

saying "thank you"? **(Scruffy whispers)**
It made you feel really good. **(Scruffy nods)**
And when we say thank you to God, I wonder how that makes Him feel. **(Scruffy whispers)**
You think that makes Him feel really happy. **(Scruffy nods)**
(Give a testimony about how saying "thank you" to God no matter what we're going through can bring us what we need - peace inside, as we trust Him.) As we say "thank you" to God, what we're saying is "I trust you", "I love you", "I know your plans for me are good ones", and if we live our lives in complete and utter trust in God then He lifts us onto a new plane. **(Scruffy whispers)**
You've never travelled on a plane. **(Scruffy nods, Scruffy whispers)**
But you think we ought to sing a "thank you" song, a love song to God.
(Announce a song)

SCRUFFY - SLAVERY

Hello Scruffy, I'm glad you're here today, I didn't ask you last time you were here if you'd been to the Gifts and Ministries day to see the deacons. **(Scruffy whispers)**
You didn't go. **(Scruffy shakes his head)**
Why was that? **(Scruffy whispers)**
You were scared. **(Scruffy nods, Scruffy whispers)**
But you did go to the subsequent evening the other week. **(Scruffy nods)**
What made you go? **(Scruffy whispers)**
It was the Easter Service. **(Scruffy nods)**
Well that's good, what particular part of the service? **(Scruffy whispers)**
It was the chocolate eggs. **(Scruffy nods vigorously)**
Oh Scruffy, so how did you get on? **(Scruffy whispers)**
You crept in just as it was beginning to get dark. **(Scruffy nods)**
Was the deacon you saw fierce? **(Scruffy shakes his head, Scruffy whispers)**
No' he seemed more nervous than you and kept looking round to see who was watching. **(Scruffy nods, Scruffy whispers)**
You had your details written down and you've been sent a report. **(Scruffy nods)**
What dose it say? **(Scruffy whispers)**
You don't know because you can't read. **(Scruffy nods and retrieves the report from his bag)**
Would you like me to read it to you? **(Scruffy nods)**

     Name: Scruffy **(Scruffy nods)**
     Gifts: Helping **(Scruffy nods)**,
          Pastoral Care **(Scruffy looks around, mouth open)**
     Abilities: Getting into pickles **(Scruffy nods)**,
          Eating **(Scruffy nods vigorously)**,
          Visual communication **(Scruffy looks around, mouth open)**
     Passions: Biscuits **(Scruffy nods)**,
          Sausages **(Scruffy nods enthusiastically)**,
          Chocolate **(Scruffy nods vigorously)**
     Current Service: Assists Sunday Worship **(Scruffy looks around, mouth open)**,
     Outreach **(Scruffy looks around, mouth open)**
     Outcome: Scruffy has developed a niche for himself in Sunday Services. **(Scruffy looks around, mouth open)** He believes he should now serve as a cleaner, **(Scruffy nods)** confirmed by the visions he has had of chocolate. **(Scruffy nods)**
Visions, Scruffy? **(Scruffy nods, Scruffy whispers)**
You've seen lots of chocolate adverts on the television! **(Scruffy nods)**
Oh, Scruffy!
The report isn't signed Scruffy, which deacon did you see?

(Scruffy whispers)
That's confidential. **(Scruffy nods, Scruffy whispers)**
You'd just like to say one thing. **(Scruffy nods)**
What's that? **(Scruffy whispers)**
Aren't our deacons wonderful? **(Scruffy nods)**
You seemed very keen on the chocolate part of the report Scruffy.
(Scruffy nods, Scruffy whispers)
It's your favourite thing. **(Scruffy nods)**
Did you know, Scruffy, that there have been reports on the
television and in the press recently, that people who collect cocoa
beans, which are used to make chocolate, are working as slaves?
(Scruffy whispers)
What are slaves? **(Scruffy nods)**
Slaves are people who have no rights, they are owned by other
people and treated as if they were property and sometimes beaten.
(Scruffy looks around, mouth open)
In fact some people are so concerned about this that they have
decided only to buy "Fairtrade" chocolate where they know the
workers are not slaves. **(Scruffy whispers)**
Can you buy "Fairtrade" Good Boy Choc Drops? **(Scruffy nods)**
I don't know, Scruffy, I'll have to try to find out. **(Scruffy whispers)**
You bet that sort of thing didn't happen in bible times.
(Scruffy nods)
Well actually, it did, Scruffy, and to God's chosen people, the
Israelites. **(Scruffy looks around, mouth open, Scruffy whispers)**
Were they picking cocoa beans? **(Scruffy nods)**
No Scruffy they were making bricks. **(Scruffy whispers)**
Why didn't God stop it? **(Scruffy nods)**
He decided to, and in such a way that they would never forget His
powers of deliverance. **(Scruffy whispers)**
Did all the brick houses fall apart? **(Scruffy nods)**
No, God chose a strong leader. He chose Moses, who at first made
all sorts of excuses to get out of the job and ended up by saying
that he couldn't speak well. **(Scruffy whispers)**
You know the problem. **(Scruffy nods)**
When Moses went to ask Pharaoh to let the Israelites go for three
days to worship God in the desert, Pharaoh became furious and as
well as saying "no", he made the slaves go and get their own straw
for the brick making and **still** expected them to make the same
number of bricks as before. **(Scruffy whispers)**
Did they get paid overtime? **(Scruffy nods)**
No Scruffy, slaves don't get paid. **(Scruffy looks around mouth open,
then whispers)**
What did God do then? **(Scruffy nods)**
He told Moses to warn Pharaoh that he would send **plagues** on his
land, Egypt, if he did not let the Israelites go. **(Scruffy whispers)**
Can plagues be itchy things - like fleas? **(Scruffy nods and shakes his
head vigorously, Scruffy whispers)**
So did he let them go? **(Scruffy nods)**

No, he didn't, until the last and most terrible plague, which was when the firstborn of all families and cattle would die. God said, "There will be loud wailing throughout Egypt - worse than there has ever been or will ever be again. But among the Israelites not a dog will bark at any man or animal." **(Scruffy whispers)**
You'd be on the Israelites' side? **(Scruffy nods, Scruffy whispers)**
So the Israelites were all right after that? **(Scruffy nods)**
Well they would have been, if they had obeyed God and lived to please Him. **(Scruffy whispers)**
So what happened to them? **(Scruffy nods)**
Lots and lots of adventures, but you'll have to come to Sunday Club to find out more. **(Scruffy whispers)**
When will you find out about your cleaning job? **(Scruffy nods)**
I think you'll have to wait until there's a vacancy, but I'm sure you'll be allowed to help so that you can start training. **(Scruffy retrieves a duster from his bag)**
What have you got there, Scruffy? It's a duster. **(Scruffy nods, Scruffy whispers)**
With static attraction for chocolate crumbs. **(Scruffy nods, Scruffy whispers)**
You bought it from a door to door salesman? **(Scruffy nods and disappears)**
Oh Scruffy!

Actually we are all slaves, slaves to the wrong things that we do in our lives, but God loves us so very much, that he has provided a way to free us and forgive us, through the death of Jesus on the cross.

We are going to sing "For God so loved the world...."
A line in it says "F is for forgiveness and now I am free"
Let us be sure that we are free because we too have God's forgiveness.

SCRUFFY - KENNEL TROUBLE

Hello Scruffy, how are you today? **(Scruffy whispers)**
You've had an exciting time? **(Scruffy nods)**
What's happened? **(Scruffy whispers)**
It's Floppy's kennel. **(Scruffy nods, Scruffy whispers)**
When it was first built, you thought it was better than yours.
(Scruffy nods and retrieves a picture of a red kennel from his bag)
Why was that? **(Scruffy whispers)**
Floppy had wall to wall carpeting. **(Scruffy nods, Scruffy whispers)**
A remote controlled water dish. **(Scruffy nods, Scruffy whispers)**
A feeding bowl with a thermostatic heater built in. **(Scruffy nods,
Scruffy whispers)**
A solar powered heating system. **(Scruffy nods, Scruffy whispers)**
And a view over the golf links. **(Scruffy nods, Scruffy whispers)**
It just wasn't fair. **(Scruffy nods, Scruffy whispers)**
You'd had your kennel for ages, and although it was in your football
team's colours, it just wasn't cool any more. **(Scruffy nods, Scruffy
whispers)**
Floppy kept saying how good his kennel was and you were sure he'd
been laughing at your one. **(Scruffy nods)**
Oh surely not, Scruffy, he is a friend of yours. **(Scruffy whispers)**
Not a close friend. **(Scruffy nods)**
Anyway tell me what happened. **(Scruffy whispers)**
There was a big storm. **(Scruffy nods, Scruffy whispers)**
The wind got stronger and stronger. **(Scruffy nods, Scruffy whispers)**
The rain started to bucket down. **(Scruffy nods, Scruffy whispers)**
You had to find your earplugs because you knew you'd never get to
sleep otherwise. **(Scruffy nods, Scruffy whispers)**
Then there was an extra strong gust of wind, a ripping sound, and a
dreadful howl. **(Scruffy nods)**
What was it, Scruffy? **(Scruffy whispers)**
Floppy's kennel was flattened. **(Scruffy nods and retrieves a picture of
a few red planks from his bag)**
But your kennel was still standing. **(Scruffy nods)**
How was that? **(Scruffy whispers)**
Your kennel was built on really strong foundations. **(Scruffy nods,
Scruffy whispers)**
But poor Floppy's kennel had been put up quickly on a patch of
sand. **(Scruffy nods, Scruffy whispers)**
Floppy howled and howled and was inconsolable. **(Scruffy nods,
Scruffy whispers)**
Try as you could, you couldn't get to sleep again. **(Scruffy nods,
Scruffy whispers)**
So in the end you just had to go and invite him to spend the rest of
the night in your kennel. **(Scruffy nods)**
That was kind of you, Scruffy. **(Scruffy nods, Scruffy whispers)**
But you made sure he had the end near the open door. **(Scruffy
nods)**

Oh, Scruffy.

Jesus said, "Everyone who hears these words of mine and does not put them into practice is like a foolish man who built his house on sand. The rain came down, the streams rose, and the winds blew and beat against that house, and it fell with a great crash."
(*Hold up the picture of the broken planks.*)
Jesus is reminding us how important it is to put our trust in Him, to make sure that our lives are "founded" in Him and that we obey His teachings.

Well Scruffy, what's happened to Floppy now? **(Scruffy whispers)**
They're taking a bit longer to build his kennel this time so you've offered to let him share yours until it's ready. **(Scruffy nods, Scruffy whispers)**
That's really kind of you, Scruffy **(Scruffy nods, Scruffy whispers)**
How much should you charge him for rent? **(Scruffy nods)**
Oh Scruffy **(Scruffy disappears back in his bag)**

Scruffy - God's Preservation of the Bible
(Jeremiah and the burning of the scrolls)

Hello Scruffy I haven't seen you in church lately, what have you been up to? **(Scruffy whispers)**
You've got a bone to pick with me? **(Scruffy nods, and retrieves an advert from his bag)**
What's this? Let me read it out. **(Scruffy reacts as I read)**
The Scruffy - back by popular demand **(Scruffy nods vigorously)**
If your carpets are reluctant to give up their bits, fluff and pet hairs to the vacuum cleaner, then Scruffy will be there to help. Especially useful around the edges of fitted carpets, stairs and a brilliant solution to pet owner's problems. Other uses include tile grouting, car ice scraper and a squeegee to wipe up spilt liquids. **(Scruffy whispers)**
You want to know why I've been advertising your services? **(Scruffy nods, Scruffy whispers)**
Cleaning up chocolate crumbs is one thing. **(Scruffy nods, Scruffy whispers)**
But you're not at all happy about tile grouting, car ice scraping, or being used as a squeegee. **(Scruffy shakes his head)**
Oh Scruffy, no, it's all right, I didn't advertise **you**, it's all about a Scruffy, a special tool, not about you. **(Scruffy looks around mouth open)**
Anyway Scruffy I've been meaning to ask you how you've been getting on at Obedience Classes. You must have been going along there for quite a time now. **(Scruffy whispers)**
You want me to get you a special lead? **(Scruffy nods)**
That's good, what's special about it? **(Scruffy whispers)**
It's got writing on it. **(Scruffy nods)**
Does it say "I am a good dog"? **(Scruffy shakes his head)**
Does it say "I have learnt to trust and obey"? **(Scruffy shakes his head)**
I give up. What does it say? **(Scruffy whispers)**
So many cats. **(Scruffy nods, Scruffy whispers)**
So few recipes. **(Scruffy nods, Scruffy laughs)**
Oh Scruffy, that's dreadful. You can't possibly need that for Obedience Classes. **(Scruffy shakes his head, Scruffy whispers)**
You just want to parade it in front of The Cat Next Door. **(Scruffy nods)**
Scruffy, that's really naughty, come on I want to know how Obedience Classes are going. **(Scruffy hangs his head)**
Oh Scruffy, what's the matter? **(Scruffy whispers)**
It's all too difficult. **(Scruffy nods, Scruffy whispers)**
You're never going to get it right. **(Scruffy shakes his head, Scruffy whispers)**
So you and Jake decided to do something about it. **(Scruffy nods, Scruffy whispers)**
Jake? Oh that's your Irish wolfhound friend, isn't it? **(Scruffy nods,**

Scruffy whispers)
Two weeks ago. **(Scruffy nods, Scruffy whispers)**
Jake knocked the instruction book on the floor. **(Scruffy nods, Scruffy whispers)**
And pushed it under the table. **(Scruffy nods, Scruffy whispers)**
All the owners were chatting, so they didn't notice. **(Scruffy shakes his head, Scruffy whispers)**
You and Jake started tearing the pages out and chewing them up. **(Scruffy nods)**
Oh Scruffy **(Scruffy whispers)**
Especially the ones about Trust and Sit and Walking to Heel. **(Scruffy nods)**
Oh Scruffy, what's so difficult about those ones? If you learn to trust and obey, it could save your life, particularly if there's danger about. **(Scruffy looks around mouth open)**
So did you get caught? **(Scruffy shakes his head, Scruffy whispers)**
You thought you were going to have a wonderful time the following week. **(Scruffy nods, Scruffy whispers)**
You were planning to tear about and stage a fight with all the other dogs. **(Scruffy nods, Scruffy whispers)**
As well as gobbling down all the Good Boy Choc Drops. **(Scruffy nods, Scruffy whispers)**
But it didn't work out that way. **(Scruffy shakes his head, Scruffy whispers)**
The trainer had got a new book. **(Scruffy nods, Scruffy whispers)**
And worse than that, the new book had even more in it. **(Scruffy nods, Scruffy whispers)**
And so you had to try all over again. **(Scruffy nods, Scruffy whispers)**
So you had to work even harder. **(Scruffy nods)**
Oh Scruffy, so your crime didn't pay? **(Scruffy shakes his head)**

The Bible is like our training manual. It has all God's instructions for saving our lives. We may try to ignore it or disobey it but it is still always there as "The Best Instructions Before Life Ends". God has made sure that His Word has been preserved for every generation, no matter what Man may do to try to destroy it.
We're not left to struggle on our own to obey it though. God gives us His Holy Spirit to be our Help and Comforter.
Jesus says in Matthew 11 verse 30, "For the yoke I will give you is easy, and the load I will put on you is light."

Well Scruffy, what are you going to do now? (Scruffy whispers)
You're in a bit of a rush? (Scruffy nods, Scruffy whispers)
Rovers are playing Spurs this afternoon and you want to be there at the start. **(Scruffy nods and retrieves his football scarf from his bag, and wave the scarf. Scruffy whispers)**
You feel very sorry for poor Kipper though. **(Scruffy nods)**
(Choose the name of a dog owned by someone in the congregation who supports an opposing team.)

Kipper? Oh you mean Kipper X? **(Scruffy nods, Scruffy whispers)**
His people support Spurs and poor Kipper has to keep his
celebrations quiet. **(Scruffy nods, Scruffy whispers)**
One thing's for sure. **(Scruffy nods)**
What's that? **(Scruffy whispers)**
We're going to thrash them! **(Scruffy nods and disappears into his bag)**

Scruffy - Change

(I have included the first part of this script even though it is specific to our church, to provide "food for thought". The important thing is to use examples which show up well known aspects of Scruffy's character so that you can say "You never change", which is Scruffy's opening for talking about Buster.)

Well, Scruffy, how are you? **(Scruffy whispers)**
You're looking forward to going to Wicksteed Park in a couple of weeks. **(Scruffy nods, Scruffy whispers)**
It's going to be a bright sunny Saturday. **(Scruffy nods, Scruffy whispers)**
Lots of green spaces to chase the ball about. **(Scruffy nods, Scruffy whispers)**
Lots of trees to investigate. **(Scruffy nods, Scruffy whispers)**
And maybe even some ducks to chase. **(Scruffy nods)**
Scruffy! **(Scruffy whispers)**
You want to know how many people are coming to join you? **(Scruffy nods)**
There aren't very many hands going up are there? **(Scruffy shakes his head, Scruffy whispers)**
You're a bit worried about that. **(Scruffy nods, Scruffy whispers)**
You want people to wave at you if they're thinking of coming to Wicksteed Park. **(Scruffy nods, Scruffy whispers)**
That's better. **(Scruffy nods, Scruffy whispers)**
You want to know how many picnics that is? **(Scruffy nods)**
Scruffy! Actually, I've got some bad news for you. **(Scruffy looks around, mouth open)**
I've been reading the small print on the Wicksteed brochure.
It says that dogs have to kept on leads at all times. **(Scruffy looks around, mouth open, Scruffy whispers)**
No playing ball. **(Scruffy shakes his head, Scruffy whispers)**
No trees. **(Scruffy shakes his head, Scruffy whispers)**
No chasing ducks. **(Scruffy shakes his head, Scruffy whispers)**
No extra picnics. **(Scruffy shakes his head)**
Oh Scruffy, tell you what, perhaps I can make an extra big picnic so that you can have seconds. **(Scruffy whispers)**
What about thirds? **(Scruffy nods)**
Scruffy, that's rather greedy isn't it? **(Scruffy looks around, mouth open)**
You might be sick in the car going back if you eat too much. **(Scruffy shakes his head)**
Anyway, you're looking very smart today, I see you've got your bow tie on. **(Scruffy whispers)**
You're going to have your photo taken? **(Scruffy nods, Scruffy whispers)**
It's a special photographic session? **(Scruffy nods, Scruffy whispers)**
You're going to appear on the church website? **(Scruffy nods)**

Scruffy, are you sure? **(Scruffy nods, Scruffy whispers)**
You want to know which is your best side? **(Scruffy nods, then turns his head from one side to the other)**
Well I could be rude here but I don't suppose I'd better. **(Scruffy looks around, mouth open)**
Mmmmm, I suppose you have used your brush today. **(Scruffy whispers)**
You've also been to the Toddlers' birthday party. **(Scruffy nods)**
Was it good? **(Scruffy whispers)**
You thought the children looked a bit small for nine. **(Scruffy nods)**
Scruffy, the children aren't nine, but the Toddler group's been going for nine years. That's why they looked small. **(Scruffy looks around, mouth open)**
Some of them made a lot of fuss of you. **(Scruffy nods, Scruffy whispers)**
And then the food came out. **(Scruffy nods, Scruffy whispers)**
But you were a bit worried because there weren't any sausages. **(Scruffy nods, Scruffy whispers)**
In fact there was nothing there for a dog to eat. **(Scruffy nods, Scruffy whispers)**
You tried a prawn cocktail crisp. **(Scruffy nods, Scruffy whispers)**
It was only fit for the cat next door **(Scruffy nods)**
Oh Scruffy. **(Scruffy whispers)**
And then you cheered up because they brought the second course round. **(Scruffy nods, Scruffy whispers)**
You were offered a whole plate of chocolate biscuits. **(Scruffy nods, Scruffy whisper)**
But then Mandy said that you were only allowed to take one. **(Scruffy nods, Scruffy whispers)**
That really took the biscuit. **(Scruffy nods, Scruffy whispers)**
Oh Scruffy you just don't change, do you? **(Scruffy shakes his head, Scruffy whispers)**
Not like Buster. **(Scruffy nods)**
Who's Buster? **(Scruffy whispers)**
You thought everyone knew Buster the bulldog. **(Scruffy nods)**
Well I don't, tell me about him. **(Scruffy whispers)**
Buster was mean. **(Scruffy nods, Scruffy whispers)**
Buster snarled. **(Scruffy draws back his lips, Scruffy whispers)**
Buster was vicious. **(Scruffy nods, Scruffy whispers)**
Buster snapped. **(Scruffy snaps, Scruffy whispers)**
Buster bit. **(Scruffy bites, Scruffy whispers)**
Buster wore a big leather collar with metal spikes sticking out of it. **(Scruffy nods)**
He sounds really frightening. **(Scruffy nods, Scruffy whispers)**
He was the hit dog for the Terrible Terrier Troup. **(Scruffy nods)**
But you said he was a bulldog! **(Scruffy whispers)**
They couldn't say no to him. **(Scruffy whispers)**
Even they were frightened of him. **(Scruffy whispers)**
Oh dear. **(Scruffy whispers)**

And if you let your shadow go across him while he was asleep.
(Scruffy nods, Scruffy whispers)
He used to wake up and try and bite you. **(Scruffy nods)**
Oh Scruffy, he does sound a nasty dog. **(Scruffy nods, Scruffy whispers)**
And then he went away. **(Scruffy nods, Scruffy whispers)**
When he came back he'd changed. **(Scruffy nods)**
What do you mean, he'd changed? **(Scruffy whispers)**
He stopped biting. **(Scruffy nods, Scruffy whispers)**
He smiled at people. **(Scruffy nods, Scruffy whispers)**
He even told you where his best bone was buried. **(Scruffy nods, Scruffy whispers)**
He started to play with the puppies in the park while their mums went off to have a chat. **(Scruffy nods, Scruffy whispers)**
And the Terrible Terrier Troup threw him out because he wasn't terrible anymore. **(Scruffy nods)**
That is a change isn't it? What had happened to him? **(Scruffy whispers)**
It was all to do with his owner. **(Scruffy nods, Scruffy whispers)**
His first owner treated him badly. **(Scruffy nods, Scruffy whispers)**
And kept him chained up a lot of the time. **(Scruffy nods, Scruffy whispers)**
He didn't give him enough food. **(Scruffy nods, Scruffy whispers)**
Or drink. **(Scruffy nods, Scruffy whispers)**
And one day a neighbour saw him being kicked. **(Scruffy nods, Scruffy whispers)**
She told the RSPCA about it. **(Scruffy nods, Scruffy whispers)**
So he was taken away and given to a new owner. **(Scruffy nods, Scruffy whispers)**
And the new owner loves and cares for him. **(Scruffy nods, Scruffy whispers)**
So he's a really happy dog now. **(Scruffy nods)**
Well that is a big change isn't it? **(Scruffy whispers)**
And he isn't chained up anymore. **(Scruffy nods, Scruffy whispers)**
His chains have been taken off. **(Scruffy nods; Scruffy retrieves a chain from his bag)**
What have you got there? Oh these were his chains were they?
Poor Buster, imagine being chained up like that. It must have been awful. **(Scruffy nods, Scruffy whispers)**

(**_To audience_**) I wonder who your owner is? Do you belong to Jesus? Because if you don't, you're in chains. Jesus loves us and when we let him come into our lives, he makes a tremendous difference because he loves us and wants the best for us in every way. We can always trust him; he'll never let us down. The evil one just wants to spoil our lives. If we don't belong to Jesus then we belong to him and that's really sad. What a difference Jesus can make, he sets us free. Through the help of his Holy Spirit who comes to live in us, we can know the peace and joy of living with our Lord.

So, Scruffy, Buster's now a much happier dog? **(Scruffy nods, Scruffy whispers)**
You were thinking about changing your owner too! **(Scruffy nods)**
But Scruffy who would understand you as well as I do? **(Scrufy looks around, mouth open, Scruffy whispers)**
That's the problem. **(Scruffy nods, Scruffy whispers)**
You're sure you could get away with a lot more with a new owner. **(Scruffy nods)**
Oh Scruffy. (***Scruffy disappears inside his bag***)

Scruffy and the Valentine

Hello Scruffy how are you? **(Scruffy whispers)**
You're fine and you want to know who enjoyed themselves at
Activity World. **(Scruffy nods and looks around)**
(Scruffy whispers) Why was it that the big people's hands went up
first? **(Scruffy nods)**
I think it was because some of the big people enjoyed themselves
even more than the children. **(Scruffy whispers)**
Why was that? **(Scruffy nods)**
I think that normally they have to sit and watch, but this time they
could really let their hair down. **(Scruffy whispers)**
You liked your Doggie bag. **(Scruffy nods)**
What did you like eating the most? **(Scruffy whispers)**
Pizza with chocolate biscuits on top. **(Scruffy nods)**
Oh Scruffy, that's disgusting. **(Scruffy whispers)**
You liked it. **(Scruffy nods)**
Did you eat ALL the contents of your Doggie bag on your own?
(Scruffy whispers)
You shared it with Jake? That was a very loving thing to do wasn't
it? **(Scruffy whispers)**
That's what you want to talk about today. **(Scruffy nods, Scruffy
whispers)**
The love that mums and dads show for their children. **(Scruffy nods,
Scruffy whispers)**
You've brought some things along to help. **(Scruffy nods and starts to
retrieve things from his bag)** Shall we see what you've got in there?
That's your dish isn't it, the one you have your dinners on? **(Scruffy
nods, Scruffy whispers)**
That's because mums and dads feed their children. **(Scruffy nods,
Scruffy whispers)**
And they make sure they take their medicine. **(Scruffy nods, Scruffy
whispers)**
And they give them baths. **(Scruffy nods)**
Do you like having baths? **(Scruffy shakes his head, Scruffy whispers)**
You like the bit at the end when you get out and shake yourself
and make everybody wet. **(Scruffy nods, Scruffy laughs, Scruffy
whispers)**
You've got something else. **(Scruffy nods and retrieves his ball from his
bag)**
That's your ball isn't it? **(Scruffy nods)** *(If you can perfect throwing
the ball for Scruffy to catch, then you could do this here. A juggling
ball is good as it is possible to get a grip on it , even with a flat
puppet's mouth.)* **(Scruffy whispers)**
That's because mums and dads play with their children. **(Scruffy
nods, Scruffy whispers)**
They give them hugs and kisses too to show that they love them.
(Scruffy nods, Scruffy whispers)
Pardon. Are you sure? **(Scruffy nods)**

They give them a Valentine's card? **(Scruffy nods, Scruffy whispers)**
You've brought one along. **(Scruffy nods and retrieves it from his bag).**
(A red heart shape on a stand up card with "God loves you" across
the middle.))
Oh Scruffy that's a very special Valentine's card isn't it. That says
God loves you. **(Scruffy whispers)**
That's because mums and dads tell their children about God's love
for them. **(Scruffy nods, Scruffy whispers)**
And they pray with them. **(Scruffy nods, Scruffy whispers)**
And they bring them to Sunday Club and to church to find out more.
(Scruffy nods)
Shall we leave this here so that everyone's reminded that God loves
them? **(Scruffy nods, Scruffy whispers)**
But you'd like your dish and ball back. **(Scruffy nods and puts them**
back in his bag and follows them in)
It's time for us to go to Sunday Cub now.

Scruffy and God's Promises

Hello Scruffy, it's good to see you. **(Scruffy emerges more fully with a party hat on his head.)**
What have you got on you head? **(Scruffy whispers)**
It's your party hat. **(Scruffy nods)**
Scruffy, why are you wearing a party hat? **(Scruffy whispers)**
You thought an anniversary was like a party. **(Scruffy nods)**
Well I suppose it is in a way, that's a good idea. **(Scruffy whispers)**
You've brought your party piece along. **(Scruffy nods)**
Scruffy, what's your party piece? **(Scruffy whispers)**
It's some jokes. **(Scruffy nods)**
You're going to tell us some jokes? All right then what's the first one? **(Scruffy whispers)**
What did the earwig say when it fell down the stairs? **(Scruffy nods)**
I don't know, what did the earwig say when it fell down the stairs? **(Scruffy whispers)**
'Ere we go. **(Scruffy nods, Scruffy laughs)**
Oh Scruffy that's dreadful! Have you got any more? **(Scruffy nods, Scruffy whispers)**
What do you get when you give a lemon to a cat? **(Scruffy nods)**
I don't know, what do you get when you give a lemon to a cat? **(Scruffy whispers)**
A sourpuss. **(Scruffy nods, Scruffy laughs, Scruffy whispers)**
That one's your favourite. **(Scruffy nods)**
I thought it might be. Scruffy, do you know any jokes other than animal ones? **(Scruffy looks around mouth open, Scruffy nods)**
You do? **(Scruffy nods, Scruffy whispers)**
You've got a special one that you think I'd like. **(Scruffy nods)**
All right then what's that? **(Scruffy whispers)**
Who designed the Ark? **(Scruffy nods)**
Well that's easy, God did. **(Scruffy whispers)**
Then God must be an architect. **(Scruffy nods)**
Oh Scruffy, I don't know, I think we'd better sit down here and see if a special song might be coming up.

(Puppet song - It's so good to be here)

(Scruffy whispers)
You thought that was very good, yes I think that everyone thought that that was very good too. Anyway Scruffy, what else have you been up to lately? **(Scruffy whispers)**
You've been trying to cross your claws behind your back? **(Scruffy nods)**
Scruffy, why have you been trying to cross your claws behind your back? **(Scruffy whispers)**
You've been watching some of the children? **(Scruffy nods, Scruffy whispers)**
If they cross their fingers behind their backs, **(Scruffy nods, Scruffy**

whispers)
when they promise something, **(Scruffy nods, Scruffy whispers)**
they don't have to keep their promise. **(Scruffy nods)**
Scruffy, that doesn't sound very good at all. **(Scruffy whispers)**
You thought it might come in useful. **(Scruffy nods)**
Scruffy, do you know, if you promise something and you don't keep
your promise, people won't trust you. **(Scruffy looks around mouth
open, Scruffy whispers)**
What about Jake, Barney and Barcus? **(Scruffy nods)**
They're your friends aren't they? **(Scruffy nods)**
Well I think especially Barcus, because he is a police dog you know.
(Scruffy looks around mouth open)
You know, Scruffy, God always keeps His promises. **(Scruffy looks
around mouth open)**
It's what you're like on the inside that counts, that makes you
someone people can trust. **(Scruffy looks around mouth open)**
I think we'd better go and listen to another song.

(Puppet song - Buried Treasure)

(Scruffy whispers)
You want to know about some of God's promises? **(Scruffy nods)**
Well I think if you look over here you can see a lovely banner that
the Jucos have made and it mentions some of the promises that
God has made to us. **(Scruffy whispers)**
You want me to tell you about some of them? **(Scruffy nods)**
OK then, God says in the bible "My God shall supply all your needs
according to his riches in Christ Jesus." **(Scruffy whispers)**
You need a designer label rug in your kennel. **(Scruffy nods)**
Scruffy, is your old rug comfortable? **(Scruffy nods, Scruffy whispers)**
Yes, but a designer label one would be more comfortable. **(Scruffy
nods)**
Scruffy, does your rug keep you warm? **(Scruffy nods, Scruffy
whispers)**
Yes, but a designer label one would keep you warmer. **(Scruffy nods,
Scruffy whispers)**
And your friends would be very impressed. **(Scruffy nods)**
Scruffy, Do you think that is really a "need" or more of a "want"?
(Scruffy whispers)
Could I tell you about another promise? **(Scruffy nods)**
All right then. There's one that says "My God shall never leave you
or forsake you." **(Scruffy whispers)**
What does forsake mean? **(Scruffy nods)**
It means that God's never going to abandon us, even if we do
something dreadful. He still loves us and wants to care for us.
(Scruffy whispers)
You can't believe the first part. **(Scruffy nods)**
What's the first part? "He will never leave you"? **(Scruffy nods)**
Why can't you believe that, Scruffy? **(Scruffy whispers)**

You can't see him. **(Scruffy nods)**

Well Scruffy, you might not be able to see him with your eyes, but He's here by the power of his Holy Spirit. Even if you can't actually see Him, God is here with us right now. **(Scruffy whispers)**

You want me to tell you about another promise? **(Scruffy nods)**

There is a word up there which says "salvation" and there's a verse in the bible, which says that everyone who calls on the Name of the Lord will be saved. **(Scruffy whispers)**

What does that mean? **(Scruffy nods)**

Well it means that if we've done something wrong, the bible tells us we deserve to die. But because God loves us so much, He's provided a way back for us. Jesus died on the cross to take our sins and if we trust Him, we can be saved and have eternal life now and when we do pass through death, we go on to be with God in Heaven. **(Scruffy whispers)**

You'd like to think about that one. **(Scruffy nods)**

While you're doing that, perhaps we'll sit here and see if there's another song coming up. **(Scruffy nods)**

(Puppet song - Jesus Always Keeps His Promises)

Scruffy (Zacchaeus - Allegory)

Well Scruffy, how are you today? **(Scruffy whispers)**
Never mind about all that. **(Scruffy nods)**
Scruffy, what do you mean? **(Scruffy whispers)**
You want to know if it's too late to put your name down for the church Golf Day? **(Scruffy nods)**
But Scruffy, you can't play golf. **(Scruffy looks around mouth open, Scruffy whispers)**
You're very experienced on a golf course. **(Scruffy nods and whispers)**
You've spent most of the summer there. **(Scruffy nods and whispers)**
You think golfers are very funny people. **(Scruffy nods)**
Why's that? **(Scruffy whispers)**
They make a lot of fuss about "birdies". **(Scruffy nods and whispers)**
And everyone knows it should be birds. **(Scruffy nods and whispers)**
And what's so special about birds, anyway? **(Scruffy nods and whispers)**
One of the golfers even shouted out about an eagle. **(Scruffy nods, Scruffy whispers)**
And you'd have thought everyone knows there aren't any eagles around here. **(Scruffy nods)**
Scruffy, what have you actually been doing on the golf course? **(Scruffy whispers)**
Playing with the golfers. **(Scruffy nods)**
In what way? **(Scruffy whispers)**
Sometimes you hide in the trees and wait for a ball to land near you. **(Scruffy nods)**
When it does, you go and bury it in the sand and hide again. **(Scruffy nods, Scruffy whispers)**
It's very funny watching them hunting for the ball. **(Scruffy nods, Scruffy laughs)**
Oh, Scruffy! **(Scruffy whispers)**
Sometimes you put extra balls out. **(Scruffy nods, Scruffy whispers)**
And then they get very cross and get into arguments about which ball is theirs. **(Scruffy nods, Scruffy whispers)**
They usually say it's the one nearest the hole, but their partner doesn't agree. **(Scruffy nods, Scruffy whispers)**
Only you know which one is right. **(Scruffy nods, Scruffy whispers)**
Sometimes you move the flags into the sand bunkers. **(Scruffy nods, Scruffy whispers)**
It's funny watching the golfers' reactions. **(Scruffy nods, laughs)**
Oh Scruffy, I think you've been very naughty. **(Scruffy looks around mouth open, Scruffy whispers)**
But you've collected a whole bag of golf balls. **(Scruffy nods, Scruffy whispers)**
You've brought it with you. **(Scruffy nods and grabs the handle of a bag previously placed nearby)**
Scruffy, that's a very big bag for such a small dog. **(Scruffy nods)**
Scruffy, there are loads and loads of golf balls in here, **(hold up a**

couple) they must be worth a lot of money. **(Scruffy nods, Scruffy whispers)**
You were thinking of selling them to buy Good Boy Choc Drops. **(Scruffy nods)**
What changed your mind? **(Scruffy whispers)**
You were hiding behind a tree one day when someone got hold of you. **(Scruffy nods)**
Oh Scruffy, who was it? **(Scruffy whispers)**
The owner of the golf course. **(Scruffy nods)**
Was he very cross? **(Scruffy shakes his head)**
No? **(Scruffy whispers)**
He was very kind and gentle. **(Scruffy nods, Scruffy whispers)**
He began to explain to you how much you had upset the golfers. **(Scruffy nods, Scruffy whispers)**
You hadn't seen it from their point of view before. **(Scruffy shakes his head, Scruffy whispers)**
You began to feel rather uncomfortable. **(Scruffy nods, Scruffy whispers)**
You began to see that the saying "Finders Keepers" isn't right. **(Scruffy nods, Scruffy whispers)**
And that anything you find belongs to somebody. **(Scruffy nods, Scruffy whispers)**
So you're going to put all the balls back on the golf course. **(Scruffy nods)**
Don't you think that would confuse the golfers all the more? **(Scruffy looks around mouth open, Scruffy whispers)**
Yes, but it would be funny watching them! **(Scruffy nods, Scruffy laughs)**
Oh Scruffy, you're impossible! **(Scruffy looks around mouth open, Scruffy whispers)**
But after listening to the golf course owner, you've decided to be good from now on. **(Scruffy nods)**
(To audience) When Jesus met Zacchaeus, he didn't have a go at him for being a cheat and a thief. He befriended him. Zacchaeus realised he needed to change and immediately started to make amends. Jesus noted his change of heart and said "For the Son of Man came to seek and to save what was lost." God's reaction to us is the same today. The bible tells us "While we were yet sinners, Christ died for us." So we can rejoice that we are not condemned but can become children of God through Jesus' death on the cross for us.
So Scruffy, if you've decided to be good why do you want to go on the church Golf Day? **(Scruffy whispers)**
It's at Barkway, so it must be for dogs. **(Scruffy nods, Scruffy whispers)**
Anyway there is the dinner. **(Scruffy nods)**
Oh Scruffy. **(Scruffy disappears inside his bag)**

(Choose a song)

Scruffy's Birthday (Christmas)

Hello Scruffy, how are you doing today? **(Scruffy whispers)**
You've had a birthday? **(Scruffy nods)**
How exciting. How old are you? **(Scruffy whispers)**
Two **(Scruffy nods, Scruffy whispers)**
But dogs years are different from human years. **(Scruffy nods)**
Of course. One human year is seven dog years isn't it? **(Scruffy nods, Scruffy whispers)**
So that makes you fourteen. **(Scruffy nods)**
You're a teenager! **(Scruffy Nods)**
Oh Scruffy, how are you finding it? **(Scruffy whispers)**
It's awful. **(Scruffy nods)**
What's the matter? **(Scruffy whispers)**
There's a girl poodle in the park who keeps winking at you. **(Scruffy nods, Scruffy whispers)**
You're not even sure that you approve of poodles. **(Scruffy shakes his head, Scruffy whispers)**
And your hormones have been playing havoc with your vocal cords? **(Scruffy nods)**
What do you mean? **(Scruffy whispers)**
You start off like Chihuahua. **(Scruffy nods, Scruffy whispers)**
Then you go all Husky. **(Scruffy nods, Scruffy whispers)**
And you end up sounding like a St Bernard! **(Scruffy nods, Scruffy whispers)**
Oh Scruffy! **(Scruffy whispers)**
And you're trying to work out what's cool and what isn't. **(Scruffy Nods)**
What do you mean? **(Scruffy whispers)**
It isn't cool to wear a coat. **(Scruffy shakes his head, Scruffy whispers)**
And so you're the coolest dog in the street. **(Scruffy nods, Scruffy whispers)**
Particularly when it's frosty. **(Scruffy nods, Scruffy whispers)**
You'd rather be un-cool so that you can get warm again. **(Scruffy nods)**
Oh Scruffy, you poor thing, but never mind, next birthday you'll be twenty-one, that's an adult. **(Scruffy looks around mouth open, Scruffy whispers)**
That's even worse. **(Scruffy Nods)**
What do you mean? **(Scruffy whispers)**
Adult spells responsibility. **(Scruffy nods, Scruffy whispers)**
When was the last time I saw an adult chasing about after a stick? **(Scruffy nods)**
Well I really don't know. **(Scruffy whispers)**
Exactly! **(Scruffy nods)**
Well Scruffy, perhaps it would be better if you stuck to human years after all. **(Scruffy nods, Scruffy whispers)**
You'd like that. **(Scruffy nods, Scruffy whispers)**

Because then you could be a terrible two and have tantrums. **(Scruffy nods)**
Oh Scruffy. **(Scruffy laughs)**
Anyway, tell me about your birthday. Did you have lots of cards?
(Scruffy shakes his head)
No? Did you have any? **(Scruffy shakes his head)**
Oh Scruffy. **(Scruffy whispers)**
Barney, Barcus and Jake did get very excited about it and sent cards to each other. **(Scruffy nods, Scruffy whispers)**
But not to you? **(Scruffy shakes his head)**
What about presents? **(Scruffy whispers)**
You did get one. **(Scruffy nods)**
What was it? *(Scruffy gets a pink knitted wrong size garment out of his bag)*
Oh Scruffy, who was it from? **(Scruffy whispers)**
From your twin aunt. **(Scruffy nods)**
What are their names? **(Scruffy whispers)**
Spic and Span. **(Scruffy nods, Scruffy whispers)**
It doesn't even fit and it certainly isn't your colour. **(Scruffy shakes his head)**
Oh Scruffy what about your friends? **(Scruffy shakes his head)**
Oh that is sad. **(Scruffy nods, Scruffy whispers)**
But they did organise a party. **(Scruffy nods)**
Oh that was good. **(Scruffy nods, Scruffy whispers)**
But they forgot to invite you. **(Scruffy nods, Scruffy whispers)**
And it wasn't until it was over that they realised that you hadn't been there. **(Scruffy nods)**
Oh Scruffy, you must be feeling so sad? **(Scruffy nods and turns his head in, while you stroke it.)**

I wonder if that's how Jesus feels when we get so busy preparing for Christmas. Christmas dose mean Christ's Birthday after all.
How awful to leave Him out of our plans and celebrations, or just to do something as a token to save our consciences and then to get on with our lives. *(Hold up a garment)* The bible tells us that God does not want us to give Him things which are an outward show, but He wants a change of our hearts – to be genuinely sorry for the wrong things in our lives and with His help to put things right. And the **real** preparations we should be making is to be ready for when He comes again; this time not as a tiny, helpless baby, but as the Lord of Glory.
Well, Scruffy have you made it up with your friends? **(Scruffy whispers)**
You're playing with them again! **(Scruffy nods, Scruffy whispers)**
But just wait until it's their birthday! **(Scruffy laughs and disappears into his bag)**
Oh Scruffy!

Scruffy and the Anger Management Course
(The work of the Holy Spirit in us)

Hello Scruffy, how are you today? **(Scruffy whispers)**
You want to know if "S" is here? **(Scruffy nods, Scruffy whispers)**
Yes, I think I can see him, he's over there, waving at you.
(Scruffy whispers)
You want to thank him for sending you a newspaper article?
(Scruffy nods, Scruffy whispers)
It's about you going on a management course. **(Scruffy nods)**
On a management course? Scruffy, are you sure? **(Scruffy nods)**
Why should you go on a management course? **(Scruffy whispers)**
So you can boss all the other dogs around. **(Scruffy nods)**
Oh Scruffy, I don't think that would make you very popular.
(Scruffy looks around, mouth open)
You could lose all your friends. I think you'd better show me the
article. **(Scruffy retrieves it out of his bag)**
Let's see what it says.
"Scruffy sent on an anger management course after terrorising
postmen." Scruffy! Have you really been terrorising postmen?
(Scruffy looks around mouth open, then nods slowly)
Scruffy that's disgraceful! **(Scruffy whispers)**
You thought postmen were fair game? **(Scruffy nods)**
Scruffy! They're not "fair game", they're perfectly normal people
and you mustn't hurt them. **(Scruffy looks around, mouth open)**
Anyway Scruffy, this doesn't say that you're going on a
management course, but on an **anger** management course. That's
something completely different. **(Scruffy whispers)**
You want to know how different? **(Scruffy nods)**
Well, an anger management course will teach you how to control
your temper, so that when you start to feel angry, you take control
and calm down. **(Scruffy looks around, mouth open, Scruffy whispers)**
No bossing other dogs around? **(Scruffy nods)**
No Scruffy. **(Scruffy opens his mouth wide, and whispers)**
No management perks? **(Scruffy nods)**
Management perks? What do you mean, management perks?
(Scruffy whispers)
Long business lunches. **(Scruffy nods, Scruffy whispers)**
Christmas bonuses of Good Boy Choc Drops.
(Scruffy nods, Scruffy whispers)
Special contracts with sausage manufacturers. **(Scruffy nods, Scruffy
whispers)**
And a box on Rovers' home ground. **(Scruffy nods)**
No Scruffy, none of those things. **(Scruffy looks around, mouth open,
then cries into my shoulder)**
But Scruffy, if you go on an anger management course, that will
actually be much better for you. **(Scruffy whispers)**
You want to know how anything could be better than a box on
Rovers' ground? **(Scruffy nods)**

Oh Scruffy, no matter how many things you get in your life, they will never make you truly happy. True happiness comes from what we're like on the inside. **(Scruffy whispers)**
You've never seen your insides and you don't think you want to.
(Scruffy shakes his head)
No Scruffy, I didn't mean it like that, I meant that if we're at peace with ourselves and with God then that is what really matters.
(Scruffy looks around, mouth open, Scruffy whispers)
You want to know how that works? **(Scruffy nods)**
When we become Christians and ask Jesus to take control of our lives, God sends His Holy Spirit to come and live inside us to change us and make us more like Jesus every day. **(Scruffy whispers)**
That sounds difficult to understand. **(Scruffy nods, Scruffy whispers)**
You're not sure you'd want anyone inside you, pulling your strings.
(Scruffy nods)
No it's not like that at all Scruffy. We still have a free choice about what we do but the Holy Spirit helps us to choose things that please God. **(Scruffy whispers)**
Like not biting postmen? **(Scruffy nods)**
Yes, that's right Scruffy, like not biting postmen. **(Scruffy whispers)**
But you enjoy biting postmen. **(Scruffy nods)**
Oh Scruffy! Sometimes wrong things are enjoyable for a time, but God's Holy Spirit will make us aware that they are wrong and we'll start to feel more and more uncomfortable if we do them. **(Scruffy whispers)**
You'd like to think about that one. **(Scruffy nods)**
I think I'd better take you along to Sunday Club so that you can learn more about God the Father, Jesus and the Holy Spirit. **(Scruffy nods)**
But before I do that, we're going to sing "All I once held dear".